WISDOM
of
THE ANCIENTS
for
TODAY

Bilingual, *pinyin* Edition

中国古代
名人名言

Compiled by Mu Zi

FOREIGN LANGUAGES PRESS

First Edition 2007

Home Page:
  http://www.flp.com.cn
E-mail Addresses:
  info@flp.com.cn
  sales@flp.com.cn

ISBN 978-7-119-05161-1
©Foreign Languages Press, Beijing, China, 2007

Published by
Foreign Languages Press
  24 Baiwanzhuang Road, Beijing 100037, China

Distributed by
China International Book Trading Corporation
  35 Chegongzhuang Xilu, Beijing 100044, China
  P.O. Box 399, Beijing, China

Printed in the People's Republic of China

目 录
CONTENTS

修 养

Cultivation

tiān xíng jiàn jūn zǐ yǐ zì qiáng bù xī
天 行 健，君 子 以 自 强 不 息；

dì shì kūn jūn zǐ yǐ hòu dé zǎi wù
地 势 坤，君 子 以 厚 德 载 物。

zhōu wén wáng
—— 周 文 王

【解读】

天道的运行刚劲强健，作为君子，应像天道的运行一样，刚毅坚卓，永不停息；大地的气势厚实和顺，作为君子，应有大地的气势，增厚美德，容载万物。

【译文】

The movement of Heaven is mighty, thus the virtuous make themselves strong and indefatigable. The Earth's state is acquiescent power, thus the virtuous possessing vast integrity uphold the outer world.

—— *King Wen of the Zhou Dynasty*

上 善 若 水 ， 水 善 利 万 物 而
不 争 。

—— 老子

〖解读〗

最大的"善"就是水，水用自己去滋润万物而不与万物相争。

〖译文〗

The highest good resembles the way of water. It rewards all yet never contends.

—— *Laozi*

dà fāng wú yú dà qì wǎn chéng
大　方　无　隅，大　器　晚　成　，

dà yīn xī shēng dà xiàng wú xíng
大　音　希　声　，大　象　无　形　。

lǎo zǐ
——老　子

【解读】

非常宽广的区域看不见边角，宏大的人材、物器一般成熟较晚，宏大的音律听上去往往声响稀薄，宏大的气势景象似乎没有一定之形。

事物达到一种极至时，往往已经超越了普通意义上的事物的含义。

【译文】

The greatest square has no corners; the greatest vessel takes longest to complete; the greatest sound can barely be heard; the greatest form is without shape.

—— *Laozi*

When matters attain perfection, they are no longer matters in the common sense.

zhāo wén dào xī sǐ kě yě
朝 闻 道 ， 夕 死 可 也 ！

kǒng zǐ
—— 孔 子

【解读】

如果一个人在早晨真正领悟了真理的真谛，那么，即使晚上就死了也值得。

【译文】

If a person learns the Way of Truth at dawn, he may die content by dusk.

—— Confucius

5

zhì shì rén rén wú qiú shēng yǐ hài rén yǒu
志 士 仁 人 ， 无 求 生 以 害 仁 ， 有

shā shēn yǐ chéng rén
杀 身 以 成 仁 。

kǒng zǐ
—— 孔 子

【解读】

那些有志向、有仁德的人，没有为了谋求生存而损害仁德的，只有献出自己的生命来成就仁德的。

【译文】

Persons of benevolence and high ideals should not, at the expense of benevolence, cling cravenly to life instead of bravely facing death. On the contrary, they will lay down their lives for the accomplishment of benevolence.

—— *Confucius*

jiàn xián sī qí yān jiàn bù xián ér nèi zì

见 贤 思 齐 焉 ， 见 不 贤 而 内 自

xǐng yě

省 也 。

kǒng zǐ
—— 孔 子

【解读】

见到有德行的人就向他看齐，见到没有德行的人就反省自身
的缺点。

【译文】

On seeing a man of virtue, try to become his peer; on seeing
a man without virtue, examine yourself to ensure you have
not the same flaws.

—— *Confucius*

sān jūn kě duó shuài yě pǐ fū bù kě duó
三 军 可 夺 帅 也 ， 匹 夫 不 可 夺

zhì yě
志 也。

kǒng zǐ
—— 孔 子

【解读】

军队可以被夺去主帅，男子汉却不可被夺去志气。

【译文】

An army may be deprived of its commander, yet a real man
cannot be deprived of his own will.

—— *Confucius*

shì　bù　kě　yǐ　bù　hóng　yì　　rèn　zhòng　ér
士　不　可　以　不　弘　毅　，任　重　而

dào　yuǎn
道　远　。

kǒng　zǐ
—— 孔 子

【解读】

要有所作为的人须有远大的抱负和坚强的意志，因为他对社会责任重大，要走的路很长。

【译文】

The scholar must possess high aspirations and deep endurance, for his responsibility is heavy and his course long.

—— *Confucius*

wǎng zhě bù kě jiàn lái zhě yóu kě zhuī
往　者　不　可　谏　，来　者　犹　可　追　。

kǒng zǐ
—— 孔　子

【解读】

已往的事情不可挽回，未来的却还来得及。

应抓住未来。

【译文】

The past cannot be revised, and the future is yet to come.

—— *Confucius*

One should seize the future.

rén wú yuǎn lǜ bì yǒu jìn yōu
人 无 远 虑 , 必 有 近 忧 。

kǒng zǐ
—— 孔 子

【解读】

人没有长远的考虑，忧患一定会很快出现。

【译文】

One who fails to see far ahead will face danger close at hand.

—— *Confucius*

sān sī ér hòu xíng

三　思　而　后　行　。

kǒng zǐ
—— 孔　子

【解读】

要经过反复考虑，然后再去做事情。

【译文】

Think thrice before you act.

—— *Confucius*

yù sù zé bù dá
欲　速，则　不　达。

—— 孔　子

【解读】

单纯追求速度，不讲效果，反而达不到目的。

【译文】

Haste makes waste.

—— *Confucius*

Cultivation 修养

yì yán chū kǒu sì mǎ nán zhuī
一 言 出 口 ，驷 马 难 追 。

kǒng zǐ
—— 孔 子

【解读】

一句话说出了口，就是套上四匹马拉的车也难追上。
意为要信守诺言。

【译文】

A word once spoken cannot be taken back, even with a
team of four horses.

—— *Confucius*

What is said cannot be unsaid. Stand by your words.

富 贵 不 能 淫 ，贫 贱 不 能 移 ，威
武 不 能 屈 。

—— 孟 子

【解读】

金钱地位不能使自己腐化堕落，贫苦穷困不能改变自己的志向，权势武力不能让自己屈服变节。

【译文】

Neither riches nor honors could corrupt him; neither poverty nor humility could shake his will; neither force nor threats could subdue him.

—— *Mencius*

rén zhī huàn zài hào wéi rén shī
人 之 患 在 好 为 人 师。

mèng zǐ
—— 孟 子

【解读】

人的毛病在于喜欢做别人的老师，但难于反省自己的不足。

【译文】

A common problem with people is that of being too eager to assume the role of teacher.

—— *Mencius*

Those who love to tell others what to do are often too conceited to see their own shortcomings.

shēng yì wǒ suǒ yù yě yì yì wǒ suǒ yù
生　亦　我　所　欲　也，义　亦　我　所　欲

yě èr zhě bù kě dé jiān shě shēng ér
也；二　者　不　可　得　兼，舍　生　而

qǔ yì zhě yě
取　义　者　也。

mèng zǐ
—— 孟 子

【解读】

生命，也是我想要的；正义，也是我想要的。（如果）生命和正义不能够同时得到，（只好）牺牲生命来保住正义。

【译文】

I cherish life, as I do righteousness. If I cannot hold onto both, I would lay down my life for righteousness.

—— *Mencius*

bù zhī ér yán bú zhì zhī ér bù yán
不 知 而 言 ， 不 智 ； 知 而 不 言 ，

bù zhōng
不 忠 。

hán fēi
—— 韩 非

【解读】

不了解某事就发表意见，是不明智的；知道某事的原委却不愿把它说出来，是不忠诚的。

【译文】

It is unwise to proffer opinions on what one does not know; it is disloyal to reserve opinion on what one knows.

—— *Han Fei*

duō xíng bú yì, bì zì bì
多 行 不 义，必 自 毙。

zuǒ qiū míng
—— 左 丘 明

【解读】

多行不合道义之事，必然自取灭亡。

【译文】

He who inflicts much injustice is doomed to destruction.

—— *Zuo Qiuming*

Cultivation

修养

rén shuí wú guò？guò ér néng gǎi shàn mò
人　谁　无　过？过　而　能　改，善　莫

dà yān
大　焉。

zuǒ qiū míng
——左　丘　明

【解读】

哪个人没有过错呢，有了过错能及时改正，就再好不过了。

【译文】

Could any person claim truthfully to be free of mistakes? It
is better to rectify mistakes in time.

—— *Zuo Qiuming*

路 漫 漫 其 修 远 兮,吾 将 上
下 而 求 索 。

——屈 原

【解读】

在追寻真理（真知）方面，前方的道路还很漫长，但我将百折
不挠，不遗余力地（上天下地）去追求和探索。

【译文】

The way was long, and swathed in gloom, as I persevered,
seeking the elusive truth.

—— *Qu Yuan*

bù fēi zé yǐ　yì fēi chōng tiān　bù míng zé
不 飞 则 已 ， 一 飞 冲 天 ； 不 鸣 则

yǐ yì míng jīng rén
已 ， 一 鸣 惊 人 。

sī mǎ qiān
—— 司 马 迁

【解读】

（这种鸟）不飞就算了，但一飞便可冲天；不鸣叫就算了，一鸣便能惊人。

此语常用来比喻一个人平时默默无闻，关键时刻却能说出惊人之语，或做出不凡业绩。

【译文】

This bird may not have flown yet, but once it does, it shall soar to the skies. It has not cried out yet, but once it does, all will be astonished.

— *Sima Qian*

Such birds symbolize unknown people who make remarkable utterances and accomplish startling feats at key moments.

táo lǐ bù yán xià zì chéng xī
桃 李 不 言 ，下 自 成 蹊 。

sī mǎ qiān
—— 司 马 迁

【解读】

桃树、李树虽不会说话，但因其花朵芬芳，果实可口，人们
纷纷去摘取，于是便自然在树下踩出一条路来。
比喻做人如果能真诚笃信，自然就会感召人心。

【译文】

Neither the peach nor plum speak, yet beneath them a clear
path is trod.

—— *Sima Qian*

A person of true worth attracts admiration.

忠　言　逆　耳　利　于　行　，　良　药　苦

口　利　于　病　。

—— 司 马 迁

【解读】

中肯的语言虽然不好听，但对你的行动却有帮助；好的药虽然吃到嘴里是苦的，但却有利于治疗疾病。

【译文】

Good medicine, though bitter to the tongue, effectively cures illnesses. Honest advice, though harsh to the ear, induces good conduct.

—— Sima Qian

rén gù yǒu yì sǐ   huò zhòng yú tài shān
人 固 有 一 死 ， 或 重 于 泰 山 ，

huò qīng yú hóng máo
或 轻 于 鸿 毛 。

sī mǎ qiān
—— 司 马 迁

【解读】

人终究免不了一死，但死的价值不同：有的人死的价值比泰山还重，而有的人死的价值比鸿毛还轻。

【译文】

Though death befalls all people alike, it may come weightier than Mount Tai or lighter than a feather.

—— *Sima Qian*

lín yuān xiàn yú shú ruò tuì ér jié wǎng
临 渊 羡 鱼 , 孰 若 退 而 结 网 。

bān gù
—— 班 固

【解读】

站在水边想得到鱼，不如回家去做个渔网来捕鱼。

【译文】

It is better to return and weave a net, than to stand by a pond longing for fish.

—— *Ban Gu*

lǎo jì fú lì zhì zài qiān lǐ liè shì mù

老 骥 伏 枥 ， 志 在 千 里 ； 烈 士 暮

nián zhuàng xīn bù yǐ

年 ， 壮 心 不 已 。

cáo cāo

—— 曹 操

【解读】

年老的千里马只能伏在马槽上，但它的雄心壮志仍然是一日驰骋千里；有远大志向的人即使到了晚年，奋发思进的雄心也不会停止。

【译文】

An old steed in the stable still dreams of the wilds; a man of action, though advanced in years, still aspires to great exploits.

—— *Cao Cao*

wù yǐ è xiǎo ér wéi zhī wù yǐ shàn xiǎo
勿 以 恶 小 而 为 之 ， 勿 以 善 小

ér bù wéi
而 不 为 。

chén shòu
—— 陈 寿

【解读】

不要因为好事小而不做，更不能因为不好的事小而去做。

【译文】

Do no evil even if only a small evil; leave no good undone even if it is small good.

—— *Chen Shou*

rì　xǐng　qí　shēn　　　yǒu　zé　gǎi　zhī　　　wú　zé
日　省　其　身　，　有　则　改　之　，　无　则

jiā　miǎn
加　勉　。

zhū　xī
—— 朱　熹

【解读】

每日反省自己，（对别人给自己指出的缺点错误）如果有，就改正；如果没有，就用来警诫和勉励自己。

【译文】

Examine yourself every day, rectify mistakes if you have made any, and be more vigilant if you have none.

—— *Zhu Xi*

hǎi nà bǎi chuān yǒu róng nǎi dà
海 纳 百 川 ， 有 容 乃 大 。

bì lì qiān rèn wú yù zé gāng
壁 立 千 仞 ， 无 欲 则 刚 。

lín zé xú
—— 林 则 徐

【解读】

大海可以容纳千百条河流，所以它才宽广；悬崖绝壁能够直立千丈，是因为它没有过分的欲望，所以才刚正、屹立不倒。

【译文】

A great ocean can accommodate hundreds of rivers, for it is open and forbearing. A sheer cliff can soar thousands of meters into the sky, for it is upright and selfless.

—— Lin Zexu

读 书
Reading

bó xué ér dǔ zhì qiè wèn ér jìn sī

博 学 而 笃 志 ， 切 问 而 近 思 。

kǒng zǐ
—— 孔 子

【解读】

既要广泛地学习并有坚定的志向，又要认真地提出疑问并联系当前情况而思索。

【译文】

Learn extensively and perseveringly, inquire sincerely and approach things practically.

—— *Confucius*

zhī zhī wéi zhī zhī bù zhī wéi bù zhī shì
知 之 为 知 之 ， 不 知 为 不 知 ， 是

zhī yě
知 也 。

kǒng zǐ
—— 孔 子

【解读】

知道就是知道，不知道就是不知道，这才是真正的"知道"。

【译文】

To know what you know, and know what you do not —
that is "knowledge."

—— *Confucius*

wēn gù ér zhī xīn kě yǐ wéi shī yǐ
温 故 而 知 新 ， 可 以 为 师 矣 。

kǒng zǐ
—— 孔 子

【解读】

复习学习过的知识，由此掌握、领会未学习过的知识，这样的人可以当老师了。

【译文】

He who reviews the old to gain knowledge of the new is fit to be a teacher.

—— *Confucius*

xué ér shí xí zhī bú yì yuè hū
学 而 时 习 之 ， 不 亦 说 乎 ？

kǒng zǐ
—— 孔 子

【解读】

学习之后时常地去温习，并且能从中学习到新的知识，不也
是件令人愉快的事情吗？

【译文】

Is it not a pleasure after all to put into practice in due time
what one has learned?

—— *Confucius*

xué ér bú yàn huì rén bú juàn
学 而 不 厌 , 诲 人 不 倦 。

kǒng zǐ
—— 孔 子

【解读】

做人要不断学习，不感到厌烦；教育学生要有耐心，不感到
疲倦。

【译文】

A person should be insatiable in learning and tireless in
teaching.

—— *Confucius*

<pre>
xué ér bù sī zé wǎng sī ér bù
学 而 不 思 则 罔 ， 思 而 不

xué zé dài
学 则 殆 。
</pre>

<pre>
                              kǒng zǐ
                          —— 孔 子
</pre>

【解读】

只注重学习而不注重思考，就有可能会被知识的表象蒙蔽而
陷于迷惑；只注重思考而不注重学习，就有可能因误入歧途
而招致疲乏和危险。

【译文】

To learn without thinking is futile; to think without
learning is dangerous.

— *Confucius*

sān rén xíng   bì yǒu wǒ shī yān   zé qí shàn
三 人 行 ，必 有 我 师 焉 。择 其 善

zhě ér cóng zhī   qí bú shàn zhě ér gǎi zhī
者 而 从 之 ，其 不 善 者 而 改 之 。

kǒng zǐ
—— 孔 子

【解读】

三个人同行，其中必定有我的老师。选择他好的方面向他学习，
看到他不好的方面就对照自己改正自己的缺点。

【译文】

As I walk alongside two others, they may serve as my
teachers. I will choose their good qualities and follow them,
see their bad qualities and avoid them.

—— Confucius

mǐn ér hào xué bù chǐ xià wèn
敏 而 好 学 , 不 耻 下 问 。

kǒng zǐ
—— 孔 子

【解读】

聪敏而又爱好学习，不把向地位、学识不如自己的人请教当作羞耻的事情。

【译文】

Endowed with a sharp mind, remain committed to and fond of learning, and seek advice humbly from anyone including your subordinates.

—— *Confucius*

shì zhě rú sī fū bù shě zhòu yè
逝 者 如 斯 夫，不 舍 昼 夜。

kǒng zǐ
—— 孔 子

【解读】

流逝的时光，就像这日夜奔腾的河水，一去不复返！

【译文】

Time keeps passing just like a flowing river, not ceasing day or night.

—— *Confucius*

fā fèn wàng shí lè yǐ wàng yōu bù zhī
发 愤 忘 食 ，乐 以 忘 忧 ，不 知

lǎo zhī jiāng zhì
老 之 将 至 。

kǒng zǐ
—— 孔 子

【解读】

发愤用功，连吃饭都忘了，（当学问上有所获益时）快乐得把
一切忧虑都忘了，连自己快要老了也未觉察。

【译文】

So diligently absorbed in learning, forgetting meals, and
with such great joys attained, forgetting all cares; in such
moods, one even forgets about growing old.

—— *Confucius*

jìn xìn shū zé bù rú wú shū
尽 信 书 ， 则 不 如 无 书 。

mèng zǐ
—— 孟 子

【解读】

完全地、不加辨别地相信书中的东西，还不如没有（读）书。

【译文】

We would rather go without books than believe everything written.

— *Mencius*

rén shēng tiān dì jiān ruò bái jū zhī guò

人　生　天　地　间，若　白　驹　之　过

xì hū rán ér yǐ

隙　，忽　然　而　已　。

zhuāng zǐ

—— 庄　子

【解读】

人类生长在天地之间，就像小白马在细小的缝隙前跑过一样，
只是一瞬间的事情。

这句话常用来比喻人生短暂或时光易逝。

【译文】

The life of a person is as short as the time it takes a tiny white horse to gallop through a narrow crevice.

—— *Zhuang Zi*

This is often used to describe the fleetingness of life and of time.

dú shū bǎi biàn qí yì zì xiàn
读 书 百 遍 ，其 义 自 见 。

chén shòu
—— 陈 寿

【解读】

读书上百遍，书中的涵义自然就能领会。

【译文】

When a book is read a hundred times, all its meaning naturally becomes clear.

—— *Chen Shou*

hào dú shū bù qiú shèn jiě měi yǒu huì
好 读 书 ， 不 求 甚 解 。 每 有 会

yì zé xīn rán wàng shí
意 ， 则 欣 然 忘 食 。

táo yuān míng
—— 陶 渊 明

〖解读〗

喜爱读书，不在字句的解释上过分下功夫，不刻意寻求深奥
的解释（而是着重领悟文中原意）。每逢读到会心处，有了一
点新的体会，便高兴得连吃饭也忘记了。

〖译文〗

Read without bookishness, yet a pure passion for learning.
Let hidden meanings dawn, forgetting meals in the pure
ecstasy.

—— *Tao Yuanming*

dú shū pò wàn juàn xià bǐ rú yǒu shén
读　书　破　万　卷　，下　笔　如　有　神　。

dù fǔ
—— 杜 甫

【解读】

读了很多书之后，写文章自然就会得心应手。

【译文】

Reading voluminously makes for a magic flow in writing.

—— *Du Fu*

业　精　于　勤，　荒　于　嬉；行　成　于
思，毁　于　随。

—— 韩　愈

【解读】

学业的精进在于勤奋刻苦，荒废于嬉戏游乐；为人行事的成功在于深思熟虑，而败毁于随波逐流（没有自己的独立思考）。

【译文】

Progress in studies comes out of diligence, and is impeded by indolence. Success comes out of forethought, while thoughtlessness leads to failure.

—— *Han Yu*

Reading

读书

师者，所以传道授业解惑也。

—— 韩愈

【解读】

老师，是为别人传授知识、教授学业、解答疑惑的人。

【译文】

It is a teacher's responsibility to foster cardinal principles, impart professional knowledge, and resolve doubt.

— *Han Yu*

dì zǐ bú bì bù rú shī shī bú bì xián yú
弟 子 不 必 不 如 师 ， 师 不 必 贤 于

dì zǐ
弟 子 。

hán yù
—— 韩 愈

【解读】

弟子不一定不如老师强，老师也不一定要比学生贤明。

【译文】

Pupils are not necessarily inferior to their teachers, nor are teachers better than their pupils.

—— *Han Yu*

dú shū zhī fǎ zài xún xù ér jiàn jìn shú

读 书 之 法 ， 在 循 序 而 渐 进 ， 熟

dú ér jīng sī

读 而 精 思 。

zhū xī

—— 朱 熹

【解读】

读书的方法在于循序渐进，在于多读和深入思考。

【译文】

The method for reading a book is to advance step by step, peruse carefully and think deeply.

— *Zhu Xi*

少　年　易　学　老　难　成　，　一　寸
光　阴　不　可　轻　。

—— 朱熹

【解读】

年轻时学习知识比较轻松，年纪大了学习就困难多了，所以一点时光都不要浪费、轻视。

【译文】

It is much easier to acquire knowledge in youth than in old age. Therefore, even a second should by no means be wasted and belittled.

—— Zhu Xi

风声 雨声 读书声，声
声入耳；国事家事天下事，事
事关心。

—— 顾宪成

【解读】

风声、雨声、读书声，声声都听在耳中；家事、国事、天下事都是我所关心的。

【译文】

Sounds of wind, of rain, of reading, all sounds dear to the ear; affairs of family, state and the world, all affairs that wring the mind.

—— Gu Xiancheng

感情
Sentiments

pín jiàn zhī zhī bù kě wàng　zāo kāng zhī qī
贫　贱　之　知　不　可　忘　，　糟　糠　之　妻

bú xià táng
不　下　堂　。

fàn yè
——　范　晔

【解读】

不应忘却贫穷时结交的朋友，不可休弃患难与共的妻子。

【译文】

Never forget those who befriended you when once poor
or unknown, and never forsake the wife who remained by
your side through times of difficulty and hardship.

——　*Fan Ye*

hǎi shàng shēng míng yuè tiān yá gòng
海　上　生　明　月　，天　涯　共

cǐ shí
此　时　。

zhāng jiǔ líng
——　张　九　龄

【解读】

大海上升起一轮明月，远在天涯海角的人，在这个所有人团聚的时刻也和我望着同一轮明月吧。

【译文】

As the bright moon rises above the seas,
All under the skies share its same soft beams.

—— *Zhang Jiuling*

Sentiments

感情

不 堪 盈 手 赠 ， 还 寝 梦

佳 期 。

—— 张 九 龄

【解读】

月光虽好，但不能捧在手上赠送给你，还是回房睡上一觉，
在梦中和你相见吧。

【译文】

Since I cannot gift you these moonbeams,
I turn in, hoping to see you in my dreams.

—— *Zhang Jiuling*

hóng dòu shēng nán guó chūn lái fā jǐ zhī
红　豆　生　南　国　，春　来　发　几　枝　？

yuàn jūn duō cǎi xié cǐ wù zuì xiāng sī
愿　君　多　采　撷　，此　物　最　相　思　。

wáng wéi
——　王　维

【解读】

红豆生长在南方，春天来的时候它会发芽生长，希望你可以多采一些，因为它是思念的象征。

【译文】

In the south the red bean grows, in springtime branches how many?
Take with you as many as can hold, to easily remind you of me.

—— *Wang Wei*

shuí yán cùn cǎo xīn　bào dé sān chūn huī
谁　言　寸　草　心　，　报　得　三　春　晖　。

mèng jiāo
——　孟　郊

【解读】

儿女像春天的小草，母亲如同三月的阳光，小草永远也报答
不了阳光给它的温暖，儿女永远也报答不完母亲的养育之恩。

【译文】

Who wrote of the small souls of grasslands dancing,

Warmth requiting the sunshine of three springs?

—— *Meng Jiao*

huán　jūn　míng　zhū　shuāng　lèi　chuí　hèn　bù
还　君　明　珠　双　泪　垂，恨　不

xiāng　féng　wèi　jià　shí
相　逢　未　嫁　时。

zhāng jí
—— 张　籍

【解读】

我流着泪水把你送的明珠还给你，我真悔恨我们的相遇不是
在我尚未出嫁的时候。

【译文】

With two pearls, two lines of tears I return;
Tears over us not meeting earlier on.

—— *Zhang Ji*

lái rú chūn mèng jǐ duō shí, qù sì zhāo
来 如 春 梦 几 多 时，去 似 朝

yún wú mì chù
云 无 觅 处。

bái jū yì
—— 白 居 易

【解读】

来的时候，如同一场片刻即逝的春梦；去的时候，就像早晨
飘飞的云彩，全无踪迹。
比喻美好的爱情来去匆匆，只给人留下惆怅和迷惘。

【译文】

Lingering no longer than a dream in spring,
Departing as clouds at dawn fleeting.

—— *Bai Juyi*

The two lines indicate that the beauty of love is transient,
only leaving behind melancholy and bewilderment.

tiān cháng dì jiǔ yǒu shí jìn cǐ hèn mián
天　长　地　久　有　时　尽，此　恨　绵

mián wú jué qī
绵　无　绝　期。

bái jū yì
── 白 居 易

【解读】

天地虽然很长久，但也会有完尽的一天，（而此生不能相守的）遗憾却是连绵不已，永无断绝的时候。

【译文】

Though Heaven is long and the Earth old, time will see their end,

While this unending sorrow goes on and on, as if forevermore.

── *Bai Juyi*

zài tiān yuàn zuò bǐ yì niǎo zài dì yuàn
在 天 愿 做 比 翼 鸟 ，在 地 愿

wéi lián lǐ zhī
为 连 理 枝。

bái jū yì
—— 白 居 易

【解读】

在天上，我们愿作比翼齐飞的鹣鹣鸟；在地上，我们甘为永
不分离的连理枝。
比喻夫妻相亲相爱、忠于爱情。

【译文】

In Heaven let us be two birds flying ever as one,
And on Earth, two trees with branches ever intertwined.

—— *Bai Juyi*

This describes the connubial affection and faithfulness of
love.

céng jīng cāng hǎi nán wéi shuǐ chú què wū
曾　经　沧　海　难　为　水　，除　却　巫

shān bú shì yún
山　不　是　云　。

yuán zhěn
——　元　稹

【解读】

经历过无比深广的沧海的人，别处的水再难以吸引他；除了
云蒸霞蔚的巫山之云，别处的云都黯然失色。
多喻指对爱情的忠诚。

【译文】

It is difficult to be water after seeing the great seas,

As difficult to be a cloud after seeing the Three Gorges.

—— *Yuan Zhen*

The two lines have been used by later generations to
describe faith in love.

Sentiments

感情

shēn wú cǎi fèng shuāng fēi yì xīn yǒu líng
身 无 彩 凤 双 飞 翼，心 有 灵

xī yì diǎn tōng
犀 一 点 通 。

lǐ shāng yǐn
—— 李 商 隐

【解读】

身上虽然没有彩凤那双可以飞翔的翅膀；但我们的心灵却像
犀牛双角之间有一条白线一样，可以相通。

【译文】

Bodies without wings to fly side by side with the vivid
phoenix,

Yet hearts for magical moments in line as the rhinoceros
horn.

—— *Li Shangyin*

xiāng jiàn shí nán bié yì nán dōng fēng wú
相 见 时 难 别 亦 难 ， 东 风 无

lì bǎi huā cán chūn cán dào sǐ sī fāng
力 百 花 残 。 春 蚕 到 死 丝 方

jìn là jù chéng huī lèi shǐ gān
尽 ， 蜡 炬 成 灰 泪 始 干 。

lǐ shāng yǐn
—— 李 商 隐

【解读】

要见一次面是那么困难，而要分别更是难舍难分；更何况是在这东风无力、百花凋零的暮春时节。（思念之情）如同春蚕吐丝，到死方休；（不能相聚的痛苦）仿佛蜡泪，直到蜡烛烧成了灰方始流尽一样。

【译文】

Time stretches out longer and crueler since you went away,
As the east wind dies down and a hundred flowers fade.
The silkworms of spring will weave until they die,
With every night the candles weeping their wicks dry.
—— *Li Shangyin*

chūn xīn mò gòng huā zhēng fā yí cùn xiāng
春 心 莫 共 花 争 发，一 寸 相

sī yí cùn huī
思 一 寸 灰 。

lǐ shāng yǐn
—— 李 商 隐

【解读】

相思之情不要与花争着开放，每一寸相思都会化为灰烬。
这句诗抒写了一位幽闺中的女子对爱情热切的追求和失意的
痛苦，既有幻灭的悲哀，也有强烈的激愤不平。

【译文】

In spring must the human heart blossom, as all other
flowers?

Of even this bright flame of love, shall there be only ashes?

—— *Li Shangyin*

The poem describes the ardent love and disappointment of
a girl living in the seclusion of her boudoir. It reflects her
melancholy and disillusionment, along with a growing sense
of injustice.

yī dài jiàn kuān zhōng bù huǐ wèi yī xiāo
衣　带　渐　宽　终　不　悔 ，为　伊　消

dé rén qiáo cuì
得　人　憔　悴 。

liǔ yǒng
——　柳　永

【解读】

（被相思折磨得）衣服都宽大了，瘦了很多，却不后悔；甘愿为思念她渐渐消瘦与憔悴。

【译文】

The robe loosening gradually as I slowly waste away,
No more regret, but anguish for her to see me this way.

—— Liu Yong

感情

dàn yuàn rén cháng jiǔ qiān lǐ gòng chán juān
但 愿 人 长 久 ，千 里 共 婵 娟。

—— 苏 轼

【解读】

只愿互相思念的人能够天长地久，即使相隔千里，也能共享
这美丽的月色。

【译文】

May we all be blessed with longevity,
Though far apart, still share the moon's beauty.

—— *Su Shi*

liǎng qíng ruò shì jiǔ cháng shí yòu qǐ zài
两　情　若　是　久　长　时　，又　岂　在

zhāo zhāo mù mù
朝　朝　暮　暮　。

qín guān
—— 秦　观

【解读】

只要两情至死不渝，又何必贪求卿卿我我的朝欢暮乐？
爱情的真正价值不会因两人的分别而受到丝毫损伤。

【译文】

If love between the pair can last through time,

Why do they have to stay together day and night?

—— *Qin Guan*

True love can never be harmed by separation.

Sentiments

感情

cǐ qíng wú jì kě xiāo chú cái xià méi
此 情 无 计 可 消 除 ， 才 下 眉

tóu què shàng xīn tóu
头 ， 却 上 心 头 。

lǐ qīng zhào
—— 李 清 照

【解读】

离别的愁苦和相思之情怎么也无法排遣，刚刚舒展开了眉头，
却又涌上了心头。

【译文】

I cannot shake this sorrow. Deeper beyond my brow, it
gnaws at my heart.

—— *Li Qingzhao*

luò huā yǒu yì liú shuǐ wú qíng
落 花 有 意 ， 流 水 无 情 。

fēng mèng lóng
—— 冯 梦 龙

【解读】

落花有意跟随流水一同漂向远方，而流水却没有依恋落花的情意。

【译文】

Shedding petals the waterside flower pines away,
While the heartless brook babbles on about unrequited love.
—— *Feng Menglong*

qíng rén yǎn lǐ chū xī shī
情　人　眼　里　出　西　施。

pú sōng líng
——　蒲　松　龄

【解读】

热恋中的人总是把自己追求的对象看成是世界上最美丽的。
西施，是中国古代四大美女之一。

【译文】

Every woman is Xi Shi in the eyes of her lover.

—— *Pu Songling*

Xi Shi was one of the four renowned beauties in ancient
China.

待人
Relationships

二人同心，其利断金；同心
之言，其臭如兰。

—— 周文王

【解读】

两个人同心同德，团结一致，力量就大，好比锋利的刀剑，可以把金属砍断；志同道合的语言，说服力强，人们就像嗅到芬芳的兰花香味，容易接受。

【译文】

Two of one mind give strength to cut gold. Words from united hearts speak fragrant as orchids.

—— *King Wen of the Zhou Dynasty*

zhī rén zhě zhì zì zhī zhě míng   shèng rén zhě
知 人 者 智，自 知 者 明 ； 胜 人 者

yǒu lì zì shèng zhě qiáng
有 力，自 胜 者 强 。

lǎo zǐ
—— 老 子

【解读】

了解别人，可以算得上智慧，了解自己，才是真正的高明；战
胜别人，可以算得上有力量，战胜自己，才是真正的强大。

【译文】

He who knows others is intelligent; he who knows himself
is wise. He who conquers others possesses might; he who
conquers himself is invincible.

—— *Lao Zi*

jǐ suǒ bú yù wù shī yú rén
己 所 不 欲，勿 施 于 人 。

kǒng zǐ
—— 孔 子

〖解读〗

自己不想要的东西，切勿强加给别人。

〖译文〗

Do not do to others what you would not have others do to
you.

—— *Confucius*

dào bù tóng bù xiāng wéi móu
道 不 同 ， 不 相 为 谋 。

kǒng zǐ
—— 孔 子

【解读】

意见或志趣不同的人，无法在一起谋划共事。

【译文】

There is little common ground for understanding between persons holding opposing views or interests.

—— *Confucius*

行人

yǒu péng zì yuǎn fāng lái bú yì lè hū
有　朋　自　远　方　来　,　不　亦　乐　乎　?

kǒng zǐ
—— 孔　子

【解读】

有志同道合的朋友从远方来看你，不是件很令人快乐的事情吗？

【译文】

Is it not a joy after all to have friends come from afar?

—— *Confucius*

yǔ péng yǒu jiāo yán ér yǒu xìn

与 朋 友 交 ， 言 而 有 信 。

kǒng zǐ
—— 孔 子

【解读】

同朋友交往，说话要诚实，要恪守信用。

【译文】

One should always be honest and faithful to one's friends.

—— *Confucius*

Relationships

jūn zǐ hé ér bù tóng xiǎo rén tóng ér

君 子 和 而 不 同 ， 小 人 同 而

bù hé

不 和 。

kǒng zǐ

—— 孔 子

【解读】

君子在人际交往中能够与他人保持一种和谐友善的关系，但在
对具体问题的看法上却不必苟同于对方；小人则习惯于在对问
题的看法上迎合别人的心理、附和别人的言论，但在内心深处
却并不抱有一种和谐友善的态度。

【译文】

The virtuous agree with others without being mere echoes.
The lesser person echoes without being in agreement.

—— *Confucius*

jūn zǐ chéng rén zhī měi　bù chéng rén
君 子 成 人 之 美 ， 不 成 人

zhī è
之 恶 。

kǒng zǐ
—— 孔 子

【解读】

君子总是与人为善，乐于帮助别人成就好事，而不会怂恿别人干坏事。

【译文】

The virtuous help others to fulfill good deeds but not evil conduct.

—— *Confucius*

jūn zǐ tǎn dàng dàng xiǎo rén cháng qī qī
君 子 坦 荡 荡 ， 小 人 长 戚 戚。

kǒng zǐ
—— 孔 子

【解读】

君子心胸宽广，小人经常忧心忡忡，斤斤计较于个人名利得失。

【译文】

The virtuous are open-minded and at ease. An inferior person is narrow-minded and ill at ease and always calculating personal gains and losses.

—— Confucius

fù mǔ zài bù yuǎn yóu yóu bì yǒu fāng
父 母 在 ， 不 远 游 ， 游 必 有 方 。

kǒng zǐ
—— 孔 子

【解读】

如果父母在世，就不该远离家乡；如果不得已要出远门，也应让父母知道自己的去处，以免父母过于牵挂。

【译文】

While one's parents are alive, one should not travel to distant places. If it is necessary to travel, there should be a clear direction.

—— *Confucius*

If children travel afar without clear reasons and direction, their parents become deeply worried.

君 子 莫 大 乎 与 人 为 善。

mèng zǐ
—— 孟 子

【解读】

君子最高的德行就是同别人一道行善。

【译文】

The supreme virtue of a person of integrity is to do good things with others.

—— *Mencius*

夫　人　必　自　侮　，然　后　人　侮　之　；家　必

自　毁　，而　后　人　毁　之　；国　必　自　伐　，

而　后　人　伐　之　。

—— 孟 子

【解读】

人必先有自取侮辱的行为，别人才侮辱他；家必先有自取毁坏的因素，别人才毁坏它；国必先有自取讨伐的原因，别人才讨伐它。

【译文】

Others will insult only after one courts insult; others will destroy a family only after it works for its own doom; others will attack a state only after it invites attack.

—— *Mencius*

fù mǔ zhī xīn rén jiē yǒu zhī
父 母 之 心 ，人 皆 有 之 。

mèng zǐ
—— 孟 子

【解读】

疼爱儿女的心情，做父母的都有。

【译文】

There are no parents who do not love their children.

—— *Mencius*

jūn zǐ zhī jiāo dàn ruò shuǐ xiǎo rén zhī jiāo
君 子 之 交 淡 若 水 ， 小 人 之 交
gān ruò lǐ
甘 若 醴 。

zhuāng zǐ
—— 庄 子

【解读】

君子之间的交情淡得像水一样，小人之间的交往甜得像甜酒一样。

比喻真正的交往不在于外在形式而在于内心的真诚。

【译文】

Friendship between the virtuous is as pure as water; the intimacy between inferiors can be oversweet like wine.

—— *Zhuang Zi*

True friendship depends on sincerity rather than superficiality.

爱 人 者 , 人 必 从 而 爱 之 ; 利 人
者 , 人 必 从 而 利 之 ; 恶 人 者 ,
人 必 从 而 恶 之 ; 害 人 者 , 人 必
从 而 害 之 。

—— 墨 子

【解读】

爱别人的，别人也必然爱他；利于别人的，别人也必然利于他；憎恶别人的，别人也必然憎恶他；残害别人的，别人也必然残害他。

【译文】

Whoever loves others is loved by others; whoever benefits others is benefited by others. Whoever hates others is hated by others; whoever injures others is injured by others.

— Mo Zi

fù cí ér jiào zǐ xiào ér zhēn xiōng ài ér
父 慈 而 教 , 子 孝 而 箴 , 兄 爱 而

yǒu dì jìng ér shùn
友 , 弟 敬 而 顺 。

zuǒ qiū míng
—— 左 丘 明

【解读】

父亲慈祥而懂得教育孩子，儿子孝顺而懂得规劝长辈，哥哥
（对弟弟）爱护而友好，弟弟（对哥哥）尊敬和顺从。

【译文】

The father is affable and educates his children appropriately;
the son is filial and counsels his elders properly; the elder
brother takes good care of and befriends his younger
brother, who pays respect to and obeys his elder brother.

—— *Zuo Qiuming*

shì wèi zhī jǐ zhě sǐ nǚ wèi yuè jǐ
士　为　知　己　者　死　，女　为　悦　己

zhě róng
者　容　。

liú xiàng
—— 刘　向

【解读】

有志之士为了了解自己、欣赏自己的人不惜付出生命；女人为了喜欢自己的人而装扮。

【译文】

A true man is ready to die for one who knows his worth; a woman is eager to beautify herself for one who touches a chord in her.

—— *Liu Xiang*

shuǐ zhì qīng zé wú yú rén zhì chá zé
水 至 清 则 无 鱼 ， 人 至 察 则

wú tú
无 徒 。

bān gù
—— 班 固

【解读】

水太清，鱼就生存不下去；人过于苛求细致，就没有人能当他的伙伴。

【译文】

Crystal clear water feeds no fish; overly critical men keep no friends.

—— *Ban Gu*

Relationships

行

人

shì   bié   sān   rì   ，   jì   dāng   guā   mù   xiāng   dài
士　别　三　日　，　即　当　刮　目　相　待　。

chén shòu
—— 陈　寿

【解读】

对于有志气的人，分别了数日后再相见，就应当擦亮眼睛重新看待他的才能。

【译文】

One aspiring to virtue should be judged in a new light when he reappears after a three-day absence.

—— *Chen Shou*

海 内 存 知 己 ， 天 涯 若 比 邻 。

wáng bó
—— 王 勃

【解读】

朋友之间只要心心相印，志同道合，即使相隔千山万水，也仿佛近在隔壁一样。

【译文】

A friend of the heart when far away brings the distance nearer.

—— *Wang Bo*

jiāo qiǎn yán shēn　jūn zǐ suǒ jiè
交　浅　言　深　，君　子　所　戒　。

sū shì
—— 苏轼

【解读】

和没有足够交情的人深谈，是不明智的。

【译文】

It is unwise to have a deep talk with a superficial acquaintance.

—— Su Shi

yǎng bú jiào fù zhī guò jiào bù yán shī
养　不　教　，父　之　过　。教　不　严　，师

zhī duò
之　惰　。

wáng yìng lín
—— 王　应　麟

【解读】

生养孩子却不加以教育，这是父亲的过错；教育学生却不严格要求，这就是做老师的懒惰了。

【译文】

Feeding without teaching is the father's flaw. Teaching without severity is the teacher's laziness.

—— *Wang Yinglin*

ér sūn zì yǒu ér sūn fú mò wèi ér sūn

儿 孙 自 有 儿 孙 福，莫 为 儿 孙

zuò yuǎn yōu

作 远 忧 。

guān hàn qīng

—— 关 汉 卿

【解读】

子孙自有他们的福分，长辈不必为子孙过于操心，也不用太担忧。

【译文】

Since children can take care of themselves after they grow up, parents need not worry too much over the future of their offspring.

—— *Guan Hanqing*

处世
Everyday Wisdom

qióng zé biàn biàn zé tōng tōng zé jiǔ
穷 则 变 ， 变 则 通 ， 通 则 久 。

zhōu wén wáng
—— 周 文 王

【解读】

事物一旦到了极限就要改变，改变就能通达，通达就能保持
得长久。

【译文】

Privation gives rise to change; change is constant; constant
innovation leads to infinite progress.

—— *King Wen of the Zhou Dynasty*

qiān lǐ zhī xíng shǐ yú zú xià
千 里 之 行 ， 始 于 足 下 。

lǎo zǐ
—— 老 子

【解读】

千里的行程，是一步一步走出来的。
一切事业均要经历积小成大的过程。

【译文】

A journey of a 1,000 miles begins with the first step.

—— Lao Zi

Things need to be accumulated incrementally before they are achieved.

gōng yù shàn qí shì bì xiān lì qí qì
工 欲 善 其 事 ， 必 先 利 其 器 。

kǒng zǐ
—— 孔 子

【解读】

要做好工作，先要使工具锋利。

【译文】

An artisan hoping to do fine work must first sharpen his tools.

—— *Confucius*

性　相　近　也，习　相　远　也。

kǒng zǐ
—— 孔 子

【解读】

人在刚出生时，性情都很相似；由于各自生存环境的不同和影响，每个人的习性就会产生差异。

【译文】

When people are born, they are similar in temperament; when they grow up, they become different due to differing environments.

—— *Confucius*

tiān jiāng jiàng dà rèn yú sī rén yě bì xiān
天 将 降 大 任 于 斯 人 也, 必 先

kǔ qí xīn zhì láo qí jīn gǔ è qí tǐ fū
苦 其 心 志, 劳 其 筋 骨, 饿 其 体 肤,

kōng fá qí shēn xíng fú luàn qí suǒ wéi
空 乏 其 身, 行 拂 乱 其 所 为,

suǒ yǐ dòng xīn rěn xìng zēng yì qí suǒ
所 以 动 心 忍 性, 曾 益 其 所

bù néng
不 能 。

mèng zǐ
—— 孟 子

【解读】

上天要委以重任于此人，必先使其心志不定，筋骨操劳，饮食不周，穷困潦倒，遭遇挫折，以此来激励和坚定他的心性，增加他的应对能力。

【译文】

Whenever Heaven bestows upon a person great responsibility, first his resolve is tested, then his muscles and bones drained, his body starved, until he is broken and broke, his every endeavor thwarted. In this way patience and endurance are formed, and all weaknesses overcome.

— *Mencius*

qiè ér shě zhī xiǔ mù bù zhé qiè ér bù
锲 而 舍 之 ， 朽 木 不 折 ； 锲 而 不

shě jīn shí kě lòu
舍 ， 金 石 可 镂 。

xún zǐ
—— 荀 子

【解读】

用刀子雕刻，刻到一半就放弃了，腐朽的木头也不会折断；坚持雕刻不停歇，就是坚硬的金子和石头都可以雕穿。

【译文】

If you give up carving half way, you will not be able to even pierce through rotting wood. Instead, if you persist in carving, you can pierce through any hard stone or metal.

—— Xun Zi

Everyday Wisdom

处世

zhòng zhì chéng chéng zhòng kǒu shuò jīn
众 志 成 城 ， 众 口 铄 金。

zuǒ qiū míng
—— 左 丘 明

【解读】

众人一心，就像坚固的城墙一样不可摧毁；众口一词，就像
烈火一样可以销熔最坚硬的金属。

【译文】

The united will of the masses becomes a fortress; the clamor
of the masses can melt gold.

—— *Zuo Qiuming*

zhì zhě qiān lǜ bì yǒu yì shī yú zhě qiān
智 者 千 虑，必 有 一 失；愚 者 千

lǜ bì yǒu yì dé
虑，必 有 一 得。

sī mǎ qiān
—— 司 马 迁

【解读】

不管多聪明的人，在思考问题的时候，都难免会出现错误；再
愚笨的人思考问题，也有考虑周全的时候。

【译文】

The wise can think a thousand times, and still make a
mistake. A fool can think a thousand times, and may set at
least one thing right.

—— *Sima Qian*

qián shì zhī bú wàng　hòu shì zhī shī

前 世 之 不 忘 ， 后 事 之 师 。

liú xiàng
—— 刘 向

【解读】

记取从前的经验教训，作为以后的借鉴。

【译文】

Previous experience and lessons can be used as a reference or warning for future actions.

—— *Liu Xiang*

qiān fū suǒ zhǐ   wú bìng ér sǐ
千　夫　所　指　，　无　病　而　死　。

bān gù
——　班　固

【解读】

品行恶劣的人，会受到众人的指责，即使没有病也会死掉。

【译文】

When a man is condemned by all, his days are numbered even if he is not ill.

—— *Ban Gu*

Everyday Wisdom

处
世

yì　rén　fēi　shēng　　xiān　jí　jī　quǎn
一　人　飞　升　，仙　及　鸡　犬　。

wáng　chōng
——　王　充

【解读】

一人得势，和他有关的人也会随之发迹，甚至包括他家养的鸡和狗。

【译文】

When a man reaches the heights, even his chickens and dogs ascend to Heaven.

—— *Wang Chong*

yáng chūn zhī qū hè zhě bì guǎ shèng míng
阳 春 之 曲 ，和 者 必 寡 ； 盛 名

zhī xià qí shí nán fù
之 下 ，其 实 难 副 。

fàn yè
—— 范 晔

【解读】

太高雅的音乐，能够理解的人肯定很少；名望很大的人，实
际的才能经常很难跟名声相符。
常用来表示谦虚或自我警戒。

【译文】

High-brow music receives little understanding from people;
Highly reputed people rarely live up to their reputations.

—— *Fan Ye*

This saying is often used to show one's modesty, or as a self-
reminder.

tài　gōng　diào　yú　　yuàn　zhě　shàng　gōu
太　公　钓　鱼　，　愿　者　上　钩　。

lì　dào　yuán
──郦　道　元

【解读】

姜太公用不挂鱼饵的直钩钓鱼，愿意被钓的鱼，会自己主动上钩。此语常被用来比喻心甘情愿地钻进别人布置好的圈套。

【译文】

Jiang Taigong fishes with a rod without barb nor bait; the fish come to him when they are ready.

── *Li Daoyuan*

This phrase is used to describe the act of walking into a trap with eyes wide open.

yǐ tóng wéi jìng kě yǐ zhèng yī guān yǐ
以 铜 为 镜 ，可 以 正 衣 冠 ；以

gǔ wéi jìng kě yǐ zhī xīng tì yǐ rén wéi
古 为 镜 ，可 以 知 兴 替 ；以 人 为

jìng kě yǐ míng dé shī
镜 ，可 以 明 得 失 。

táng tài zōng
—— 唐 太 宗

【解读】

以铜为镜，可以看到自己的衣冠是否整齐；以古为镜，可以看到自己所作所为是否符合社会历史的发展规律；以人为镜，可以知道自己行为的得失。

【译文】

Using bronze as a mirror, we appraise how we adorn ourselves; looking through the glass of history, we can understand why empires arose and declined; through the mirror of others' rise and fall, we shall know what and what not to do.

—— *Emperor Taizong of the Tang Dynasty*

ěr rú mù rǎn bù xué yǐ néng

耳 濡 目 染 ， 不 学 以 能 。

hán yù
—— 韩 愈

【解读】

经常听到、看到，无形之中就能够受到影响，即使不学也会了。

【译文】

One is imperceptibly influenced by what is constantly seen and heard; even if without ever studying it, one will know how to do it.

—— *Han Yu*

shān chóng shuǐ fù yí wú lù liǔ àn huā
山　重　水　复　疑　无　路，柳　暗　花

míng yòu yì cūn
明　又　一　村　。

lù yóu
——陆　游

【解读】

一重重山，一道道水，正在疑惑是否无路可行之时，忽见绿柳成荫，花色明丽，一个村庄出现在眼前。

常用来比喻某些事情陷入绝境之时，忽然又有了转机。

【译文】

Just as the weary traveler despairs of finding a road through endless mountains and rivers,

A village appears and shady willows and riotous flowers beckon.

—— Lu You

This verse is often used as an allegory that things suddenly turn for the better after being mired for a long time.

万 事 俱 备 ，只 欠 东 风 。

luó guàn zhōng
—— 罗 贯 中

【解读】

所有的事都准备好了，只差刮起东风。

三国时周瑜计划火攻曹操，一切都准备就绪，只欠东风还没有刮起来，不能放火。比喻一切都已俱备，只差最后一个重要条件。

【译文】

Thousands of preparations made ready, all that is needed is the east wind.

—— *Luo Guanzhong*

During the Three Kingdom Period (220-280), Zhou Yu (175-210, a general of the Kingdom of Wu) planned to attack Cao Cao with fire. Everything was ready except the east wind needed to fan the flames. All is on hand except what is crucial.

江 山 代 有 才 人 出 ，各 领 风

骚 数 百 年 。

—— 赵 翼

【解读】

每个不同的时代，都会有人才不断出现。

【译文】

Rivers and mountains spring forth new genius with each age,
Enhancing history for centuries to come.

—— *Zhao Yi*

shì shì dòng míng jiē xué wèn rén qíng liàn
世　事　洞　明　皆　学　问　，人　情　练

dá jì wén zhāng
达　即　文　章　。

cáo xuě qín
—— 曹 雪 芹

【解读】

透彻了解世界上的事情就是学问，熟悉通达人情世故就是文章。

【译文】

A profound understanding of commonplace affairs is genuine knowledge; a mastery of worldly wisdom is true learning.

— *Cao Xueqin*

xīn bìng zhōng xū xīn yào yī jiě líng hái shì
心 病 终 须 心 药 医, 解 铃 还 是

jì líng rén
系 铃 人 。

cáo xuě qín
—— 曹 雪 芹

【解读】

治疗心理的疾病，就要用对症的药；只有那个把金铃系到老虎脖子上面去的人，才能够把金铃解下来。

常用来说明处理好一件事情，需要追根求源，找出关键症结所在。

【译文】

Only medicine to soothe the heart can a heartache cure.
Only the one who attached the golden bell to the tiger's neck can the bell untie.

—— *Cao Xueqin*

This sentence implies that to properly solve a problem requires seeking the root of the problem.

Everyday Wisdom

处世

bù jīng yí shì　bù cháng yí zhì
不 经 一 事 ，不 长 一 智 。

cáo xuě qín
—— 曹 雪 芹

【解读】

不经历一件事情，就不能增长对那件事情的见识和应对的智慧。常用于鼓励人们要积极地去尝试各种事情，就算失败了也是一种宝贵的经验。

【译文】

Without experiencing the matter yourself, you cannot obtain knowledge and insight into it.

—— *Cao Xueqin*

This is often used to encourage people to venture. Even if you fail, it would be a valuable experience.

bù jīng yì fān hán chè gǔ zěn dé méi huā
不 经 一 番 寒 彻 骨，怎 得 梅 花

pū bí xiāng
扑 鼻 香 。

féng mèng lóng
—— 冯 梦 龙

【解读】

梅花要不是经受住一次次冰雪风霜摧折之苦，哪会有清新沁人的
芳香。
在中国文化中，梅花一直是品质高洁、坚忍不屈精神的象征。这
句话是勉励人克服困难、立志成就事业。

【译文】

Plum blossoms would not have such a refreshing and
pleasant fragrance without enduring snows, storms, wind
and frost.

—— *Feng Menglong*

In Chinese culture, plum blossoms are a symbol of noble
and unyielding character. This adage is used to encourage
people to achieve success without fear of difficulty.

处

世

tà pò tiě xié wú mì chù dé lái quán bú
踏 破 铁 鞋 无 觅 处 ，得 来 全 不

fèi gōng fū
费 功 夫 。

féng mèng lóng
—— 冯 梦 龙

【解读】

急需的东西费了很大周折找，没有找到，却在无意中得到了。

【译文】

There are things that one tries everything to gain, but endless efforts end up in vain; however, sometimes you obtain something without trying to look for it — serendipity, or even inspiration.

—— *Feng Menglong*

政治

Politics

ān ér bú wàng wēi cún ér bú wàng wáng
安 而 不 忘 危 ， 存 而 不 忘 亡 ，

zhì ér bú wàng luàn
治 而 不 忘 乱 。

zhōu wén wáng
—— 周 文 王

【解读】

（真正有远见卓识的人）太平安定时不会忘记危难困苦的日子，得以生存时不会忘记灭亡的危险，国家安定时不会忘记发生变乱的可能。

【译文】

In times of peace, do not forget dangers; though surviving, do not forget downfall; during times of stability, do not forget turmoil.

—— *King Wen of the Zhou Dynasty*

tiān wǎng huī huī shū ér bù shī
天 网 恢 恢 ， 疏 而 不 失 。

lǎo zǐ
—— 老 子

【解读】

天道像一张广阔的大网，它看起来似乎很不周密，但最终不会放过一个坏人。

【译文】

Heaven's net weaves slowly but surely; those who commit crimes will be eventually punished.

—— *Lao Zi*

Politics 政治

mín bú wèi sǐ nài hé yǐ sǐ jù zhī
民 不 畏 死，奈 何 以 死 惧 之 ？

lǎo zǐ
—— 老 子

【解读】

人民不怕死，又怎么能用死来威胁他们呢？
统治者应善待百姓，让他们安居乐业。

【译文】

If people are unafraid of death, then how can they be
threatened with death?

—— *Lao Zi*

This means that a ruler should treat people well, providing
them a peaceful place to live and work.

qí shēn zhèng bú lìng ér xíng qí shēn bú
其 身 正 ，不 令 而 行 ；其 身 不

zhèng suī lìng bù cóng
正 ，虽 令 不 从 。

kǒng zǐ
—— 孔 子

【解读】

为政之人若一身正气，则不用严刑苛责，下边的人也能各行
其事；如果作风不正，则虽三令五申，众人也不会听从。

【译文】

If the ruler acts properly, the common people will obey
him without being ordered to; if he acts improperly, the
common people will not listen to him no matter how strict
the rules.

—— *Confucius*

mín wéi guì shè jì cì zhī jūn wéi qīng
民 为 贵 ，社 稷 次 之 ，君 为 轻 。

mèng zǐ
—— 孟 子

【解读】

人民是第一位的，国家其次，君主在最后。

【译文】

People are the most precious, the country second, and the ruler the last.

—— *Mencius*

dé dào zhě duō zhù shī dào zhě guǎ zhù
得 道 者 多 助 ， 失 道 者 寡 助 。

mèng zǐ
—— 孟 子

【解读】

施行"仁政"、坚持道义的君主，必定会得到多数人的拥护、支持与帮助；反之，则一定会陷入孤立无援的境地。

【译文】

A ruler exercising benevolence and justice will surely win the support and help of most people; if he fails to do so, the people will be absolved of all loyalty to him.

—— *Mencius*

Politics

政治

tiān shí bù rú dì lì dì lì bù rú rén hé
天　时　不　如　地　利，地　利　不　如　人　和。

mèng zǐ
—— 孟　子

【解读】

在战争中，良好的天气时令，不如地势有利；地势有利，不如人心一致，士气旺盛。

现多用于说明人心向背对事业成败起着决定性的作用。

【译文】

Heaven's fortune is not equal to earthly advantages; and earthly advantages are not equal to people's unity.

—— *Mencius*

This is mostly used to demonstrate that the support of people plays a decisive role in the success of any undertaking.

lè mín zhī lè zhě mín yì lè qí lè yōu
乐 民 之 乐 者 ，民 亦 乐 其 乐 ；忧

mín zhī yōu zhě mín yì yōu qí yōu
民 之 忧 者 ，民 亦 忧 其 忧 。

mèng zǐ
—— 孟 子

【解读】

如果（国君）把百姓的快乐作为自己的快乐，那么百姓也会把
国君的快乐当作自己的快乐；如果（国君）把百姓的忧愁作为
自己的忧愁，百姓也会把国君的忧愁当作自己的忧愁。

【译文】

(If a ruler were to) take people's happiness as his own
happiness, and the people will take his happiness as their
happiness; (if a ruler were to) take people's worries as
his own worries, the people will take his worries as their
worries.

—— *Mencius*

Politics 政治

shàng yǒu hào zhě xià bì yǒu shèn yān

上 有 好 者 , 下 必 有 甚 焉

zhě yǐ

者 矣 。

mèng zǐ

—— 孟 子

【解读】

地位高的人有什么喜好，那么在下面的人为了迎合这种喜好，必定会变本加厉。

【译文】

Whatever the superior is fond of, will be sought after by his followers even more.

—— *Mencius*

一 年 之 计，莫 如 树 谷；十 年 之
计，莫 如 树 木；终 身 之 计，莫 如
树 人 。

—— 管 仲

〖解读〗

想在一年内获得利益的，不如种植粮食；想在十年内获得成果的，不如种植树木；想实现国家发展的，不如培养人才。

〖译文〗

If you want to profit in one year, nothing is better than growing grain. If you want to harvest in ten years, nothing is better than planting trees. If a country wants to grow rapidly, nothing is better than cultivating talent.

—— *Guan Zhong*

cāng lǐn shí zé zhī lǐ jié yī shí zú zé zhī
仓 廪 实 则 知 礼 节, 衣 食 足 则 知

róng rǔ
荣 辱 。

guǎn zhòng
—— 管 仲

【解读】

粮仓充实，百姓才懂得礼节制度；衣食丰足，百姓才知道荣誉耻辱。

治理国家最要紧的并不是无休止的道德说教，而是要让百姓安居乐业。

【译文】

Only when the granaries are full can people learn rites and etiquette. Only when people are adequately fed and clothed can there be honor and shame.

—— *Guan Zhong*

The most important thing in running a country is to provide people a peaceful place to live and work, rather than empty and ceaseless moral lessons.

知 己 知 彼 , 百 战 不 殆 。

—— 孙 子

【解读】

既了解敌人，又了解自己，才可以永远立于不败之地。

【译文】

If you know the enemy and know yourself, you can fight a
hundred battles without a single defeat.

—— *Sun Zi*

Politics

政治

tóu zhī wáng dì ér hòu cún xiàn zhī sǐ dì
投 之 亡 地 而 后 存 , 陷 之 死 地

rán hòu shēng
然 后 生 。

sūn zǐ
—— 孙 子

【解读】

作战时把军队布置在无路可退的境地，士兵就会奋勇前进，杀敌取胜。

【译文】

Place your army in mortal peril, it shall then survive.
Thrust it into dire straits, it will then emerge safely.

—— *Sun Zi*

bǎi zhàn bǎi shèng fēi shàn zhī shàn yě
百 战 百 胜 ， 非 善 之 善 也 ；

bú zhàn ér qū rén zhī bīng shàn zhī shàn
不 战 而 屈 人 之 兵 ， 善 之 善

zhě yě
者 也 。

sūn zǐ
—— 孙 子

【解读】

每次战斗都能够取得胜利，并不是最高明的；不动用一兵一
卒，而又能降服敌人，才是高明中最高明的。

【译文】

To fight a hundred battles and win a hundred is not supreme
excellence; what would be more supreme is breaking the
enemy's resistance without fighting.

—— *Sun Zi*

Politics

政治

wéi zhèng zhě bù shǎng sī láo bù fá sī yuàn
为　政　者，不　赏　私　劳，不　罚　私　怨。

zuǒ qiū míng
——左　丘　明

【解读】

执政者不能以个人的好恶得失，来奖赏对自己有利的人或惩罚对自己有怨的人。

【译文】

A ruler should not honor favorites nor punish critics, according to his own personal feelings.

—— *Zuo Qiuming*

yùn chóu wéi wò zhī zhōng ， jué shèng qiān lǐ
运 筹 帷 幄 之 中 ， 决 胜 千 里

zhī wài
之 外 。

sī mǎ qiān
—— 司 马 迁

【解读】

帐幕里的出谋划策，决定千里之外战斗的胜利。
帷幄中的决策绝不会逊色于战场上的骁勇，甚至更加重要。

【译文】

Plan strategies within a command tent, and ensure victory on the battlefront a thousand *li* away.

— *Sima Qian*

Strategies made in a command tent are no less important than fighting in the battlefield; in reality, they are even more important.

Politics

政治

xiān fā zhì rén hòu fā zhì yú rén
先 发 制 人 , 后 发 制 于 人 。

bān gù
—— 班 固

【解读】

在军事、政治斗争中，首先要掌握主动权，才能战胜对方，否则就会为对方所控制。

【译文】

In a military or political fight, one should forestall the enemy, or end up controlled by the enemy.

—— *Ban Gu*

jū gōng jìn cuì sǐ ér hòu yǐ

鞠 躬 尽 瘁 ，死 而 后 已 。

zhū gě liàng
—— 诸 葛 亮

【解读】

我将谨慎勤勉，尽心尽力去完成职责，一直到死。

【译文】

Bend one's back to a task, and stop only after death.

—— *Zhuge Liang*

Politics

政治

xiān tiān xià zhī yōu ér yōu hòu tiān xià zhī

先 天 下 之 忧 而 忧 ， 后 天 下 之

lè ér lè

乐 而 乐 。

fàn zhòng yān

——范 仲 淹

【解读】

在天下人忧虑之前忧虑，在天下人快乐之后快乐。

【译文】

Be the first under heaven to worry about state affairs, and the last to enjoy oneself.

—— *Fan Zhongyan*

人 生 自 古 谁 无 死，留 取 丹 心

照 汗 青。

—— 文 天 祥

【解读】

自古以来，人终不免一死！但死得要有意义，倘若能为国尽忠，
死后仍可光照千秋，青史留名。

【译文】

No one can live forever; let me die with a loyal heart
shining through the pages of history.

—— *Wen Tianxiang*

tiān xià xīng wáng pǐ fū yǒu zé
天 下 兴 亡 , 匹 夫 有 责 。

mài mèng huá
—— 麦 孟 华

【解读】

国家兴盛或衰亡，每个普通的人都有责任。

【译文】

Everyone has a duty towards his country; everyone is responsible for its fate.

—— *Mai Menghua*

哲 理
Philosophy

huò xī fú zhī suǒ yǐ fú xī huò zhī

祸 兮 福 之 所 倚 ，福 兮 祸 之

suǒ fú

所 伏 。

lǎo zǐ

—— 老 子

【解读】

祸是造成福的前提，而福中又会含有祸的因素。

【译文】

Good fortune lies within bad, bad fortune lurks within good.

—— *Lao Zi*

bù yǐ guī jǔ bù néng chéng fāng yuán
不 以 规 矩, 不 能 成 方 圆 。

mèng zǐ
—— 孟 子

【解读】

木匠如果不用画圆的仪器圆规和画方形的仪器曲尺，就画不
成标准的圆形和方形。

在这个世界上并不存在不受任何限制的自由，无论做什么事
情都需要遵循一定的标准和法则。

【译文】

If a carpenter uses no compass nor ruler, he cannot draw
standard circles and squares.

—— *Mencius*

Unlimited freedom does not exist in the world; everything
must follow certain rules and standards.

Philosophy

哲理

āi mò dà yú xīn sǐ
哀 莫 大 于 心 死 。

zhuāng zǐ
—— 庄 子

【解读】

一个人最大的悲哀莫过于心情沮丧、意志消沉到不能自拔、完全麻木的地步。

【译文】

Nothing causes greater sorrow than despair.

—— *Zhuang Zi*

táng　láng　bǔ　chán　　huáng　què　zài　hòu
螳　螂　捕　蝉　，　黄　雀　在　后　。

zhuāng　zǐ
——　庄　子

【解读】

螳螂捕捉知了，却不知道黄雀正在它身后要吃它。

这句话用来形容那些目光短浅、一心图谋侵害别人，却不知自己也正被别人算计的人。

【译文】

The mantis stalks the cicada, unaware of the oriole waiting in the backdrop.

—— *Zhuang Zi*

This image describes those shortsighted people wanting to hurt others, unaware of greater lurking dangers.

Philosophy 哲理

qīng   qǔ zhī yú lán   ér qīng yú lán   bīng
青 ， 取 之 于 蓝 而 青 于 蓝 ； 冰 ，

shuǐ wéi zhī ér hán yú shuǐ
水 为 之 而 寒 于 水 。

xún zǐ
—— 荀 子

【解读】

青色染料是从蓝草里提炼出来的，但颜色比蓝草更深；冰是
由水形成的，但是比水寒冷。

【译文】

Indigo blue is extracted from the indigo plant but it is bluer
than the plant itself; ice is formed by water but it is colder
than water.

—— *Xun Zi*

bù dēng gāo shān bù zhī tiān zhī gāo yě

不 登 高 山 ， 不 知 天 之 高 也；

bù lín shēn yuān bù zhī dì zhī hòu yě

不 临 深 渊 ， 不 知 地 之 厚 也。

xún zǐ
—— 荀 子

【解读】

不登上高山就不知道天有多高，不下深谷就不知道大地有多厚。

【译文】

One will not know how high the sky, without ascending the summit of a mountain; nor will one know how deep the earth, without descending a deep valley.

—— *Xun Zi*

liú shuǐ bù fǔ hù shū bú dù
流 水 不 腐 ， 户 枢 不 蠹 。

lǚ bù wéi
—— 吕 不 韦

【解读】

流动的水不会发臭，经常转动的门轴不会腐烂。

【译文】

Running water is never foul, and a door-hinge in use never gets worm eaten.

—— *Lü Buwei*

pí zhī bù cún   máo jiāng yān fù
皮 之 不 存 ， 毛 将 焉 附 ？

zuǒ qiū míng
—— 左 丘 明

【解读】

皮都没有了，毛往哪里依附呢？

【译文】

With the skin gone, what can the hair attach to?

—— *Zuo Qiuming*

Philosophy

哲

理

yù jiā zhī zuì hé huàn wú cí
欲　加　之　罪，何　　患　无　辞。

zuǒ qiū míng
——左　丘　明

【解读】

要想加罪于人，不愁找不到罪名。

【译文】

When out to condemn someone, some charge can always be trumped up.

—— *Zuo Qiuming*

千 丈 之 堤，以 蝼 蚁 之 穴 溃；百
尺 之 屋，以 突 隙 之 烟 焚。

—— 韩 非

【解读】

千里大堤，会因小小蝼蚁打洞而决口；百尺高楼，也会被烟囱的缝隙进出火星引起火灾而焚毁。

【译文】

One ant-hole may cause the collapse of a miles-long dike; a spark from a chimney may ignite a fire destroying a mile-high house.

—— *Han Fei*

Philosophy 哲理

yù bàng xiāng zhēng yú rén dé lì

鹬 蚌 相 争 ，渔 人 得 利 。

liú xiàng
—— 刘 向

【解读】

水鸟和河蚌互相争斗，最终获得好处的是旁边观战的打渔人。

【译文】

When the snipe and the clam struggle, it is the fisherman who stands to benefit.

—— *Liu Xiang*

sài wēng shī mǎ ān zhī fēi fú

塞 翁 失 马 ，安 知 非 福 ？

liú ān
—— 刘 安

【解读】

边塞上的老翁丢了一匹马，谁知道这不会是一件福事呢？
这句话比喻一时虽然受到损失，也许反而因此能得到好处。

【译文】

When the old man on the frontier lost his mare, who could
have guessed it was a blessing in disguise?

—— *Liu An*

This fable tells people that sometimes a small loss may end
up positive.

Philosophy

哲 理

yí yè luò zhī tiān xià qiū
一　叶　落　知　天　下　秋 。

liú ān
——刘　安

【解读】

从一片树叶的凋落，知道秋天的到来。

【译文】

The falling of a single leaf heralds the coming of autumn.

—— *Liu An*

bǐ yì shí yě cǐ yì shí yě qǐ kě
彼 一 时 也 ， 此 一 时 也 ， 岂 可

tóng zāi
同 哉 ？

bān gù
—— 班 固

【解读】

这个时候与以前的那个时候情况大不一样，怎么可以同等看待呢？

具体问题要具体分析。一个人在不同的位置上，他的价值就不一样；一件事放在不同历史阶段，对它的评价也会发生变化。

【译文】

That was then, this is now; how can things be perceived in the same way?

— Ban Gu

Different things should be treated in different ways. One's worth changes with one's position. Views on the same thing change during different periods of history.

Philosophy 哲理

bǎi wén bù rú yí jiàn
百　闻　不　如　一　见 。

bān gù
——班　固

【解读】

听别人讲一百次，不如亲眼见一次。

【译文】

It is better to see once than to hear it a hundred times.

—— *Ban Gu*

chā ruò háo lí   miù yǐ qiān lǐ
差 若 毫 厘 ， 谬 以 千 里 。

dài shèng
—— 戴 圣

【解读】

倘若起始就有细微的偏差，就会越来越偏离既定目标，酿成
大错。

【译文】

One early small discrepancy of an inch can end up in an
error of a thousand miles.

—— *Dai Sheng*

bú rù hǔ xué yān dé hǔ zǐ
不 入 虎 穴 ， 焉 得 虎 子 。

fàn yè
—— 范 晔

【解读】

不进老虎窝，怎能捉到小老虎。

比喻不亲历险境、不经过艰苦的实践，就不能取得重大的成就。

【译文】

How can one catch tiger cubs without walking boldly into the tiger's lair?

—— *Fan Ye*

This implies that one cannot obtain great success without experiencing hardships oneself.

shè rén xiān shè mǎ qín zéi xiān qín wáng
射 人 先 射 马 ，擒 贼 先 擒 王 。

dù fǔ
—— 杜 甫

【解读】

射杀敌人，要先射敌人骑的马；捉拿敌人，要先抓住敌人的
头领。

这句话常用来比喻办事情要抓住重点、抓住要害。

【译文】

When shooting a man, first shoot his horse;

When fighting with the enemy, first catch their leader.

—— *Du Fu*

This line from a poem explains that one should focus on the
essential points when tackling a problem.

Philosophy

哲理

chén zhōu cè pàn qiān fān guò　bìng shù qián
沉　舟　侧　畔　千　帆　过　,　病　树　前

tóu wàn mù chūn
头　万　木　春　。

liú yǔ xī
—— 刘 禹 锡

【解读】

沉船旁边，成千上万的船只驶过；枯树面前，成千上万的树木生机盎然。

比喻虽然历经坎坷，但仍然应该看到前途的光明。

【译文】

A thousand sails pass alongside a sunken ship;

Ten thousand flowers bloom beneath the stricken tree.

—— *Liu Yuxi*

This verse from Tang-Dynasty poet Liu Yuxi's poem was to encourage himself to keep his spirits high and look forward to a brighter future, even when old and after experiencing great hardship.

wèn qú nǎ dé qīng rú xǔ wéi yǒu yuán tóu
问　渠　哪　得　清　如　许，为　有　源　头

huó shuǐ lái
活　水　来。

zhū xī
—— 朱 熹

【解读】

想问：那水渠中的水为什么总是这样清澈？原来，是水的发源处源源不断地流过来新鲜的水。

【译文】

Why is the stream so limpid?
It is ever fresh from the source.

—— Zhu Xi

Philosophy 哲理

bù shí lú shān zhēn miàn mù zhǐ yuán shēn
不 识 庐 山 真 面 目，只 缘 身

zài cǐ shān zhōng
在 此 山 中 。

sū shì
—— 苏 轼

【解读】

　　为什么不能辨认庐山的真实面目呢？只因为身在庐山之中。

【译文】

Why can I not identify great Mount Lu?

It is because I have stood myself right on the mountain.

—— *Su Shi*

qiǎo fù nán wéi wú mǐ zhī chuī
巧 妇 难 为 无 米 之 炊 。

lù yóu
—— 陆 游

【解读】

再聪明的主妇，没有米也做不出饭来。

【译文】

Even the smartest housewife cannot cook without rice.

—— *Lu You*

Philosophy

哲理

zhòng guā hái dé guā　zhòng dòu hái dé dòu
种　瓜　还　得　瓜　,　种　豆　还　得　豆。

shī nài ān
—— 施 耐 庵

【解读】

种下瓜的种子就会收获瓜，种下豆的种子就会收获豆。

【译文】

Plant melons and you get melons; sow beans and you get beans.

—— *Shi Nai'an*

liú dé qīng shān zài   bú pà méi chái shāo
留　得　青　山　在　，　不　怕　没　柴　　烧　　。

líng méng chū
——　凌　蒙　初

【解读】

只要青山还在，就不怕没有柴草烧火。

比喻只要还有时间，就有将来和希望。

【译文】

As long as there are green mountains, one need not worry
about firewood.

—— *Ling Mengchu*

As long as there is life, there is hope and future.

Philosophy

哲

理

dāng jú zhě mí páng guān zhě qīng
当　局　者　迷　，　旁　观　者　清　。

liú è
—— 刘　锷

【解读】

当事人被碰到的事情搞糊涂了，旁观的人却很清醒。

【译文】

From within, one is lost;

From outside, one can see clearly.

—— *Liu E*

An outsider sees things more clearly than one imprecated.

索引
Index

图书在版编目（CIP）数据

中国古代名人名言：汉英对照 / 木子编著．
—北京：外文出版社，2007
ISBN 978-7-119-05161-1
Ⅰ．中… Ⅱ．木… Ⅲ．汉语—对外汉语教学—语言读物
Ⅳ．H195.5

中国版本图书馆 CIP 数据核字（2007）第 174943 号

英文翻译：李 洋 欧阳伟萍
英文审定：May Yee Kris Sri Bhaggiyadatt 郁 苓
责任编辑：杨春燕 李建安
装帧设计：华子图文
印刷监制：张国祥

中国古代名人名言

木 子 编著

ⓒ 外文出版社
出　　版：
外文出版社出版（中国北京百万庄大街 24 号）
邮政编码　100037
外文出版社网址：www.flp.com.cn
外文出版社电子信箱：
info@flp.com.cn sales@flp.com.cn
印　　刷：
北京外文印刷厂
发　　行：
中国国际图书贸易总公司发行（中国北京车公庄西路 35 号）
北京邮政信箱第 399 号　邮政编码：100044
2007 年（小 16 开）第 1 版
2007 年第 1 版第 1 次印刷
（汉英）
ISBN 978-7-119-05161-1
05600
10-CE-3858P